Maria Wiesmüller

Austrian Pastries and Desserts

80 Recipes

KOMPASS Kitchen Delights

Before you begin!

Austrian cuisine is world-renowned for its "Mehlspeisen," or pastries. The main ingredient for these delicacies is flour and other flour products, along with several other ingredients.

Although some of the sweet, as well as savory, pastries can also be served as entrées, we usually think of pastries as desserts. Some of the desserts, namely the delectable cakes, originate from the French "pâtisserie," the fine art of pastry-making.

Every Austrian province boasts its own specialties. Many of these are known well beyond the provincial borders, for example Viennese Apple Strudel, Salzburger Nockerln, Linzer Torte or Sachertorte.

Besides flour, many of the recipes call for baker's cheese, eggs, milk and cream. Compotes or fruit sauces provide the necessary vitamins and minerals.

Austrian desserts are therefore quite nutritious. Strudel, pancakes and sweet dumplings, "Schöberl" (fruit fritters), "Palatschinken" (Austrian crêpes), and other dishes with yeast are all traditional delicacies.

It is always important to precisely follow the preparation techniques. The introduction contains many helpful tips. The recipes themselves are easy to follow and illustrated with mouth-watering photographs. They are grouped into warm and cold desserts, the latter supplemented with instructions for the basic preparation of different, basic types of dough and batter.

One distinct advantage of all these recipes is that

almost all are made with high-quality, low-cost, readily accessible ingredients. Moreover, no special culinary tools are needed, because all the preparations can be made with equipment on hand.

I hope you enjoy my culinary tour of Austrian desserts and that you delight in trying out the recipes of this beautiful country.

Sincerely,
Maria Wiesmüller

Contents

Page

Warm Desserts

Cold Desserts

Traditional Austrian Desserts – At a Glance

All the "warm desserts" are, as the name says, warm, and served fresh from the oven or skillet. The most popular of these is the **strudel,** which is made with different fillings typical to the region. A potato dough is the base for delicious **dumpling** dishes ("Knödel," "Nudeln," "Nocken"), each filled differently and served with all sorts of sauces. Not to be forgotten are the **fritters and doughnuts,** which in bygone days were often served only on holidays. "Pafesen" filled with "Powidl" (plum jam) or traditional ruffles are just two examples. Those desserts **prepared on the stovetop** include **"Palatschinken"** (Austrian crêpes) with various fillings. **"Schmarrn"** are another favorite and include the celebrated Emperor's Pancake ("Kaiserschmarrn"). Hailing from the region of Salzburg, but well-known beyond those borders, is **"Salzburger Nockerln,"** a delicate soufflé of flour, egg yolks, sugar and beaten egg whites. In many regions of Austria, you will also find **puddings** and **soufflés,** foremost being the archetypal "Scheiterhaufen" bread pudding. The "cold desserts" include all **cookies** and **cakes** made from a wide variety of doughs and batters (yeast dough, rich egg pastry, sponge-cake, torte and coffee cake). Last but not least are the easy-to-make **creams** and **sweet sauces.** Particularly the sweet sauces are served with many types of warm desserts, as they add complimentary flavor, color and nutrients.

About the Basic Ingredients

Flour:

In preparing pastries and desserts, we mainly use a white wheat flour and/or non-wheat flour like potato, corn or rice flours. The proteins known as gluten found in wheat flour are especially absorbent and make a dough elastic. Doughs like rich egg pastry or strudel dough, which are prepared without rising agents (baking powder or yeast) must stand before proceeding so that the proteins can be activated. Non-wheat flours do not possess gluten and are therefore not a substitute in elastic dough. However, with batters rich in eggs like spongecake, wheat flour can be partly replaced with a non-wheat flour. The finished product will then be finer in texture. Salt improves the absorption ability of the gluten and, thus, should always be added to the pastry in small amounts (1 pinch).

Milk and Cream:

Every type of commercially available milk, whether whole milk or skim milk, is appropriate for making pastries and desserts. However, skim milk is preferred because of its high protein content. For baking, the milk should be lukewarm or at least room temperature. For stove-top desserts, the milk should be heated to a boil in a pot rinsed with cold water.

Cream has at least 30% butter fat. It is used in liquid form or well-chilled and whipped. For best results, add sugar before whipping or use powdered sugar, which dissolves better.

Fats:

Butter plays an important role in pastry-making. It is comprised of approx. 82% fat, 16% water, some lactic acid, lactose, vitamins and salt. Butter adds a distinct flavor to all dishes and therefore can only sometimes be substituted with margarine. For rich egg pastry, work in sliced, chilled butter. For dough with baking powder, however, the butter should be soft. Remember to remove it from the refrigerator early enough. Butter should never be over-heated in sauces or too browned as it will taste bitter.

Margarine, preferably vegetable oil-based, is primarily used for cold desserts like cookies. It also has a fat content of 80% and, thus, is often used for cooking. Margarine is not, however, a replacement for butter, but rather an individual ingredient on its own.

Lard and **vegetable shortenings** are an important ingredient in Austrian pastries and desserts. Numerous recipes call for these fats not only in the dough, but also to fry different pastries like doughnuts, ruffles or fritters. Their tolerance to temperature is also important.

Oil is also occasionally used as a cooking fat or is used to brush dough. If oil is used as a substitute, it should be high in unsaturated fats, such as: sunflower oil, soybean oil or wheatgerm oil.

Baker's Cheese:
In dessert and pastry recipes that call for fresh baker's cheese, use the reduced-fat variety. It is important that the cheese be relatively dry. You should therefore drain it in a sieve or a dish towel. Smoked baker's cheese is made with buttermilk or milk from Alpine pastures. This special ingredient is popular in the province of Salzburg.

Eggs:
Eggs are indispensable for all dessert and pastry dishes. They bind on the one hand, and loosen on the other. They should always be fresh and of the same size (i.e. grade A = 2 oz). When creaming, eggs should have the same temperature as the butter to avoid lumping. When separating eggs,

make sure that the egg whites are free of all traces of yolk, because the slightest fat from the yolk will prevent the whites from beating. It is equally important that the mixing bowl and whisk also have no fat on them.

Rising Agents and Flavorings:

The leavening of the dough is essential to the success of many pastries and desserts. To achieve this, use **yeast,** for example, which gives all baked goods a distinct taste. Good yeast must always be fresh, recognizable by its gold-gray color and its moist cake form. **Baking powder** is a mixture of bicarbonate of soda, tartaric acid and starch. It is ideal for all baked goods, especially those with a longer baking time. It must be added just before baking.

Nuts – whole, chopped or ground – are used in many pastries and desserts. **Almonds** are also irresistible. Lightly toasting them in the oven or blanching them makes the skin easy to peel.

Walnuts have a wonderful aroma but are aroma-sensitive and should therefore be stored separately. Sweet-tasting **pistachios** may be substituted for almonds. **Grated coconut**, available in dried form, is essential for the popular "Busserl" (macaroons). **Vanilla** is the queen of baking spices. Made from scratch by scraping out the vanilla bean and mixing with sugar, it is most aromatic. **Dried** fruit like pears, apricots, raisins, sultanas and currants should be thoroughly rinsed and towel-dried before use.

REPUBLIK ÖSTERREICH

BURGENLAND

KÄRNTEN

NIEDERÖSTERREICH

Ober-
terreich
Jpper Austria)
Linz
Nieder-
österreich
St. Pölten
(Lower Austria)
WIEN
(Vienna)
Eisenstadt
Burgen-
land
Steiermark
(Styria)
Graz
ärnten
Carinthia)
Klagenfurt
0
50 km
EICH
SALZBURG
STEIERMARK
TIROL

Preparation Tips

1. Use only the best ingredients, that means: fresh milk, butter, eggs, nuts and lemon zest. Weigh or measure the exact amount called for in the recipe beforehand. Carefully separate eggs. All the ingredients, including liquids, should be at room temperature for best results.

2. Flour should always be sifted so that it is light and should be mixed with baking powder last.

3. Prepare the appropriate baking dishes, sheets and cake pans ahead of time. They may be greased and then dusted with flour or bread crumbs or wiped with water. Baking paper, cut to fit, works just as well.

4. All equipment like scales, measuring cups, mixing bowls, food processors or electric mixers should be readily accessible.

5. The kitchen must be warm and free of drafts when preparing yeast dough. The dough must always have enough time to rise.

6. The oven should be properly preheated, if required. This is particularly crucial for delicate desserts like Salzburger Nockerln.

Strudel

Basic Recipe:

1 cup flour

pinch of salt

1 1/2 T melted butter or 2 T oil

1 egg

approx. 1/2 cup lukewarm water

some butter, oil or margarine

softened butter to brush on strudel

● Sift flour into a bowl. Make a well in the center. Add salt, butter or oil and the egg, beaten. Knead to a soft, smooth dough. Add water gradually until the dough forms a medium-firm ball. Continue to knead by hand until the dough is no longer sticky, but has a silky sheen. As you knead, slap the dough several times onto a floured pastry board, until it is completely smooth and supple. Then form a ball, brush with oil, cover and let stand for at least 30 minutes.

● Meanwhile prepare the filling. Roll the dough out approx. 1/4 inch thick onto a floured cloth and, using a rolling pin, roll the dough out gently from the center. Place the backs of your hands under the dough and carefully lift and stretch it until it is as thin as tissue paper. Cut off thicker edges.

● Use the trimmed edges to "patch" any holes.

● Distribute the filling over the dough. Fold sides of

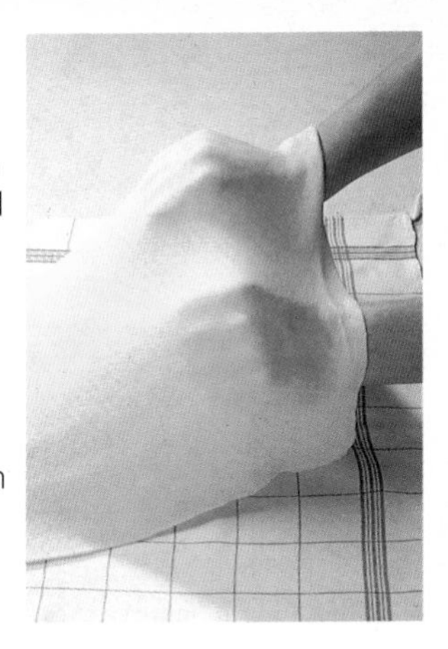

dough in over filling. Using cloth, roll the dough jelly-roll fashion.

● Use the cloth to slide the strudel onto a greased baking sheet, brush with butter and bake approx. 45-55 minutes in a preheated oven at 400°-425° F until golden brown. Brush occasionally with butter.

Viennese Apple Strudel / Alt-Wiener Apfelstrudel

Strudel dough – see recipe p. 10

Filling:

1/3 cup raisins

2 T rum

3 lb baking apples

just over 1/2 cup sugar

pinch of ground cinnamon

In Addition:

1/2 cup bread crumbs

some flour

3 1/2 oz butter

sifted powdered sugar

- Prepare basic strudel dough from the ingredients given and let stand for 30 minutes.

- Meanwhile prepare the filling. Rinse and dry the raisins; then drizzle rum over them and let stand. Peel, remove core and thinly slice the apples. Stir in sugar and cinnamon, combined.

- Spread a large cloth on a table and sprinkle with flour. Roll the dough out very thin, moving gently from the center out, using the backs of your hands. Cut off the thicker edges.

- Preheat the oven to 400°–425° F. Grease the baking sheet.

- Sprinkle bread crumbs on dough and cover 2/3 of the dough with apple filling and raisins. Fold sides of dough in over filling and, using the cloth, gently roll dough jelly-roll fashion. Use the cloth to slide strudel onto baking sheet. Brush with butter.

- Bake approx. 45–60 minutes in a preheated oven at 400°–425° F. Brush occasionally with butter. Serve warm, dusted with powdered sugar.

Cheese Strudel / Topfenstrudel

(Lower Austria)

Strudel dough – see recipe p. 10

Filling:

2 egg whites

2 T softened butter

2 egg yolks

1/2 cup sugar

1 tsp vanilla extract

just over 2 cups baker's cheese

1/2 cup cream

1/2 cup raisins

3-4 baking apples

juice of 1/2 lemon

In Addition:

butter or oil for pan

4 T melted butter

2 T sifted powdered sugar

● Prepare basic strudel dough from the ingredients given and let stand approx. 30 minutes. Roll onto a large cloth.

● Beat egg whites for filling. Cream butter with egg yolks, sugar and vanilla until frothy. Gradually add the drained baker's cheese and the cream alternately. Stir in raisins and peeled, cored and thinly sliced apples as well as lemon juice.

● Grease the baking sheet and preheat oven to 350°–400° F.

● Fold beaten egg whites into the cheese mixture and spread over strudel dough, leaving some space on the edges. Fold the sides of dough in over filling and, using the cloth, roll the strudel and slide it onto the baking sheet.

● Brush with butter and bake approx. 50–60 minutes. Brush occasionally with remaining butter.

● Remove the strudel from the oven when ready and let cool slightly, approx. 20 minutes. Slice and serve with a generous dusting of powdered sugar.

Cherry Strudel / Kirschstrudel (Tyrol)

Strudel dough – see recipe p. 10

Filling:
2 lb fresh or canned cherries, pitted

2/3 cup sugar

3-4 T sugar

2/3 cup bread crumbs

2-3 T very soft butter

2 T sifted powdered sugar

● Prepare basic strudel dough from the ingredients given. Cover and let stand.

● Meanwhile, wash cherries, pat dry and remove pits. Melt butter in a large skillet and toast the bread crumbs until light brown. Spread a large cloth on a table and sprinkle with flour. Roll the dough out very thin and stretch it gently from the center out using the backs of your hands until it is as thin as tissue paper.

● Brush with softened butter. Sprinkle 2/3 of the dough with bread crumbs and top with cherries. Mix sugar and cinnamon and sprinkle on top. Using the

cloth, roll the strudel jelly-roll fashion. Place strudel in a greased roasting pan or baking sheet and brush with remaining butter.

- Bake approx. 45-55 minutes in a preheated oven at 400°–425° F until golden brown. While still warm, dust with powdered sugar, if desired, and serve immediately.

Styrian Grape Strudel / Steirischer Weintraubenstrudel

Dough:

1 1/4 cups flour
1 egg
pinch of salt
2–3 T oil
approx. 1/2 cup lukewarm water
1–2 T oil

Filling:

approx. 1 1/2 lb fresh grapes
3 1/2 oz butter
2/3 cup bread crumbs
3–4 T sugar
1/3 cup ground almonds
pinch of cinammon, optional
1 tsp vanilla extract
2–3 T softened butter
2 T sifted powdered sugar

- Sift flour into a bowl. Make a well in the center. Add salt, oil and the egg, beaten. Knead to a soft, smooth dough. Add water gradually until the dough forms a medium-firm ball. Continue to knead by hand until the dough is no longer sticky, but has a silky sheen. Then form a ball, cover and let stand for at least 30 minutes.
- Meanwhile rinse the grapes and pat dry; if desired, halve and seed. Melt butter in a large skillet and toast the bread crumbs until light brown.
- Combine sugar, almonds, cinnamon and vanilla.
- Spread a large cloth on a table and sprinkle with flour. Roll the dough out very thin and stretch it

gently from the center out using the backs of your hands until it is as thin as tissue paper. Cut off thicker edges.

- Preheat the oven to 400°–425° F.
- Brush the dough with butter. Sprinkle 2/3 of the dough with bread crumbs and top evenly with grapes. Sprinkle the sugar and almond mixture on top. Fold the sides of dough in over filling and, using the cloth, roll the strudel and slide it onto a greased baking sheet. Brush with remaining butter.
- Bake approx. 45–60 minutes or until golden brown. Brush occasionally with butter. Serve with a generous dusting of powdered sugar.

Cream Strudel from Ebensee / Ebenseer Millirahmstrudel

(Upper Austria) Strudel dough – see recipe p. 10

- 5–6 slices of dried white bread or 5–6 dried bread rolls
- 1 cup warm milk
- 4 oz butter
- 1/2 cup sifted powdered sugar
- juice of 1/2 lemon
- 4 eggs
- pinch of salt
- 1 cup sour cream
- 1/3 cup raisins
- 4 T butter
- approx. 1 cup hot milk

- Cut crusts off bread. Soak in milk, press excess milk out and put through a sieve or food mill. Cream butter with sugar, lemon juice, egg yolks and salt. Stir in bread mass and sour cream. Beat egg whites until stiff; fold into batter.
- Spread batter onto strudel dough. Sprinkle with raisins and roll jelly-roll fashion. Place in a greased pan, brush with melted butter and bake at 400°–425° F approx. 50–60 minutes. After the first 20–25 minutes of baking, pour hot milk over strudel.

Dumplings

Basic Preparation:

When preparing dumplings, it is important that they be boiled in a large enough pot with as much depth as possible and approx. 2 qt salted water.
After gently dropping dumplings into the boiling water, reduce heat to a gentle simmer. Be consistent with the size of the dumplings and make sure they are not piled on top of each other. They are done when they float to the top of the water. Little log-shaped dumplings should simmer approx. 6–8 minutes, and standard potato-dough dumplings, 8–10 minutes depending on their size. Other dumplings made from baker's cheese take 10–15 minutes.

Apricot Dumplings / Burgenländer Marillenknödel (Burgenland)

Dough:

- approx. 1lb potatoes, cooked
- pinch of salt
- 1/2 cup flour
- 2 T semolina
- grated rind of 1/2 lemon
- 2 T butter
- 2 egg yolks

Filling:

- approx. 1 lb fresh or canned apricots, pitted
- 5-6 sugar cubes
- 8 T butter mixed with sugar and just over 1/2 cup bread crumbs

● Boil, peel and rice the baking potatoes. Combine potatoes with salt, flour, semolina, soft butter and egg yolks and mix in a mixing bowl to form a smooth dough. Let stand approx. 30 minutes.

● Wash apricots and press out pits. Replace pit with half a sugar cube. Form a 2 1/2-inch-thick roll and cut into 3/4-inch-thick slices. Flatten each slice somewhat and place apricot in center. Fold dough over fruit and roll to form a ball.

● Gently drop the dumplings into 2 qt lightly salted water. Bring to a boil, then reduce heat and simmer for 8-10 minutes. Meanwhile brown the bread crumbs in the melted butter. Remove dumplings with a slotted spoon and roll in bread crumbs. Dust with powdered sugar and serve immediately.

Poppy–Seed Dumplings / Kärntner Mohnnudeln (Carinthia)

Potato dough – see "Apricot Dumplings"

some flour
4 T softened butter
1/2 cup ground poppy seeds
3–4 T sifted powdered sugar

● Prepare dough as described for "Apricot Dumplings." Heat plenty of lightly salted water. Form dough into a thick roll. Cut nut-sized pieces and form these into 3–3 1/2-inch-long, log-shaped dumplings. Cook in water over low heat for 6–8 minutes.

● Toast poppy seeds in butter. Remove dumplings with a slotted spoon and dredge in poppy seeds. Dust with powdered sugar.

Blueberry Dumplings / Moosnocken

(Salzburg)

- approx. 1 lb blueberries
- 1 1/4 cups flour
- pinch of salt
- 2 T sugar
- 1–2 cups hot milk
- approx. 8 T butter

● Rinse blueberries and pat dry with towel. Combine flour, salt, sugar and berries and mix thoroughly.

● Gradually add warm milk until mixture forms a soft dumpling dough. Melt butter in a large skillet. Use a spoon to scoop out dumplings and transfer to skillet. Flatten the dumplings somewhat and brown both sides.

Plum Pockets / Powidltascherln

(Lower Austria) Potato dough – see "Apricot Dumplings"

- 2/3 cup plum jam
- 1–2 tsp sugar
- pinch of ground cinnamon
- 2 T rum
- 1 egg white
- 4 T butter
- 3 T bread crumbs
- 2 T sifted powdered sugar

● Prepare dough as described for "Apricot Dumplings." Mix plum jam with sugar and cinnamon. Roll dough out thinly on a floured surface and cut out circles about 3 inches in diameter. Brush edges with egg white. Place a tsp of plum filling in the center of each circle. Fold over and press edges firmly together. Simmer in salted water approx. 7–9 minutes. Brown bread crumbs in butter. Transfer pockets from water to skillet with a slotted spoon and dredge in bread crumbs. Sprinkle with powdered sugar and serve.

Cheese Dumplings with Plum Compote / Topfenknödel mit Zwetschgenröster (Burgenland)

just over 2 cups baker's cheese, 4 eggs

1/2 cup bread crumbs

1/2 cup sugar, pinch of salt

1 tsp vanilla extract

1/2 cup bread crumbs, toasted in 4 T butter

1 lb fresh or canned plums, pitted, 2 T sugar

pinch of ground cinnamon

1 T rum, 1 T lemon juice

● Drain baker's cheese and, in a bowl, mix with eggs, bread crumbs, sugar, salt, and vanilla until smooth. Let stand approx. 45 minutes.

● Wet hands and form small dumplings. Drop into boiling, salted water and reduce heat; gently simmer approx. 10 minutes. Remove dumplings with a slotted spoon and transfer to skillet. Dredge in buttered bread crumbs.

● Rinse plums and cut in half, removing pits. Cook in a small skillet with sugar, cinnamon, rum and lemon juice. Serve separately.

Cherry Pockets / Kirschmandeltascherln (Carinthia)

Dough:

- approx. 1 lb potatoes, cooked
- pinch of salt
- 1/2 cup flour
- 2 T semolina
- 2 T softened butter
- 2 egg yolks
- grated rind of 1/2 lemon

Filling:

- just over 1 cup fresh **or** canned cherries, pitted
- 1/2 cup sugar
- 3–4 T water
- 2 T butter
- 2 tsp flour
- some milk
- 1 egg white
- 3 T butter
- 3 T bread crumbs
- 1 T sifted powdered sugar

● Boil potatoes with skin; peel and rice while warm. Let cool. Combine salt, flour, semolina, butter, egg yolks and lemon zest in a mixing bowl; stir until smooth. Let stand approx. 30 minutes.

● Rinse cherries and remove pits. Boil with sugar and some water. In a saucepan, make a roux of flour and butter; add a few tablespoons of milk. Boil to thicken, stirring constantly. Add to cherries as a binder and let cool.

● Roll potato dough out thinly on a floured surface and cut 2 1/2-inch circles. Brush edges with egg white. Place a teaspoonful of cherry mixture in center, fold dough over to make pocket and press edges together firmly.

● Bring 2 qt lightly salted water to a boil. Gently drop pockets in, reduce heat and simmer gently for 8-11 minutes. Remove with a slotted spoon and dredge in toasted bread crumbs. Dust with powdered sugar and serve.

Apple Dumplings from the Lavant Valley / Lavanttaler Apfelknödel

(Carinthia)

4 large apples (approx. 1 lb)	approx. 2/3 cup flour
1/4 tsp salt	4 T softened butter
1 egg, lightly beaten	1/4 cup sugar
	1 tsp ground cinnamon

● Peel, core and dice or grate apples; mix well with salt, beaten egg and sifted flour.

● Knead until smooth and let stand at least 1 hour.

● Bring salted water to a boil.

● Wet hands and form dumplings; drop gently into boiling water and reduce heat. Simmer approx. 10-15 minutes, depending on size. Remove with a slotted spoon.

● Melt butter and stir in sugar and cinnamon. Pour over dumplings and serve immediately.

Sweet Cheese Dumplings / Süsse Topfennocken (Tyrol)

- 5–6 T softened butter
- 2 T sugar
- 3 eggs, pinch of salt
- just over 2 cups baker's cheese
- 3/4 cup semolina
- 3 T raisins
- 6 T bread crumbs, toasted in 5–6 T butter

● Cream butter, sugar, eggs and salt. Stir in baker's cheese, semolina and raisins and let stand approx. 30 min.

● Bring salted water to a boil. Reduce heat. Using a spoon dipped in the hot water, scoop out dumplings and drop them into the water. Gently simmer approx. 10–15 minutes. Remove carefully and arrange on plates.

● Brown bread crumbs in a skillet with melted butter and sprinkle over the dumplings. Serve with cherry compote.

Doughnuts and Fritters Basic Preparation:

Each province has its own unique pastries passed down for generations. These pastries are made from various doughs or batters and in a form typical to the region. It is important to use heat-tolerant and water-free **fats** like vegetable shortening, oil or butter-flavored shortening. After frying, the fat should be purified. Use a coffee filter or a sieve lined with a paper towel to filter out impurities in the oil. For frying, the **pan** should be wide and deep enough so that you can fill it (half-full) with approx. 3 1/2 inches of oil. The pastries should freely float in the pan without touching each other. The **temperature of the frying oil** is also important.

The ideal temperature is 350° F. To check the temperature, drop in a bit of batter. If it forms bubbles, the temperature is right.

Do not place too many pastries in the hot oil at once. After frying, the pastries should be placed on paper towels to drain. They taste best served fresh.

Tyrolean Doughnuts / Ziachkiachl

- 2 cups flour
- 1/2 cup lukewarm milk
- 1/2 package active dry yeast
- 1 T sugar
- 3 egg yolks
- 3–4 T softened butter
- grated rind of 1/2 lemon
- approx. 1 cup milk
- shortening or oil
- cranberry jam
- 2 T sifted powdered sugar

● Sift flour into a mixing bowl and make a well in the center. Crumble yeast in and stir with some milk and sugar. Cover and let rise approx. 30 minutes in a warm place. Add egg yolks, butter, lemon zest and remaining milk to the dough. Knead dough until smooth and does not stick to sides of bowl.

● Let rise again approx. 15–20 minutes. Roll out onto a floured surface and cut out equal portions and form balls; let rise.

● Heat oil for frying. Using your hands, stretch balls to make a well in the center (illus. p. 25). Fry, turning once.

● Drain and cool. Fill the well with your favorite jam, if desired.

Battered Plum Jam Sandwiches / Pafesen (Lower Austria)

- 5–6 slices of dried white bread **or** 5–6 dried bread rolls
- 3/4 cup plum jam
- 5 T flour
- 2/3 cup milk
- 2 eggs
- 2 T cream
- pinch of salt
- 1/2–2/3 cup bread crumbs
- 5–7 T shortening
- 5 T sugar, mixed with 1/2 tsp ground cinnamon

● Scrape crust from rolls and slice. Spread one half with plum jam and cover with a slice of plain bread. Press together firmly. Turn in flour to coat both sides. Sprinkle evenly with milk and wait for it to be absorbed.

● Meanwhile heat shortening in a skillet and beat eggs with cream and salt.

● Dip bread slices first in egg mixture, then in bread crumbs and fry immediately over moderate heat.

● Sprinkle with cinnamon and sugar; serve warm.

Fried Semolina Dumplings / Gebackene Griessknödel

(Upper Austria)

2 cups milk

2 T butter

1 T sugar

pinch of salt

1/2 cup semolina

2 eggs

pinch of ground nutmeg

In Addition:

2–3 T bread crumbs

shortening or oil

● Bring milk, butter, sugar and salt to a boil. Add semolina and stir until the batter does not cling to sides of pan. Cool slightly and alternately fold in egg yolks, nutmeg and beaten egg whites.

● Using two spoons cut a large dumpling from the dough. Let cool slightly; simmer approx. 10–12 minutes.

● Dredge dumplings in bread crumbs and fry until golden.

Our Tip:
Apricot sauce is a good accompaniment to "Fried Semolina Dumplings." See p. 91 for recipe.

Rhine Valley Pastry Pillows / Rheintaler Walerküachle (Vorarlberg)

- 1 1/4 cups flour
- 5–6 T softened butter
- 1 egg, pinch of salt
- 1/4 cup cream
- 2–3 T cold milk
- shortening or oil
- 5 T sugar, mixed with 1/2 tsp ground cinnamon

● Combine sifted flour, softened butter, egg and salt; add some cream and chilled milk to form a firm dough. Knead until air bubbles appear. For best results, use a food processor or electric mixer. Let stand approx. 30 minutes.

● Use a rolling pin to roll dough out max. 1/4-inch thick on a pastry board and cut into large squares with a pastry cutter.

● Moderately heat oil and fry the "pillows" on each side. Remove and sprinkle with a mixture of cinnamon and sugar.

Our Tip:
Pear compote is a delicious accompaniment. See recipe p. 95.

Apple Fritters / Apfelschöberl

(Burgenland)

1/2 cup milk	3–4 medium-sized apples
2 eggs, pinch of salt	shortening or oil
2/3 cup flour	2–3 T sugar

● Blend milk, eggs, salt and flour to make a thick batter. Wash and core apples; cut into approx. 3/4-inch-thick slices or wedges. Dip in batter and immediately fry in butter or shortening until golden brown.

● Remove with a slotted spoon and sprinkle with sugar.

Our Tip:
In the same fashion, you can make fritters with elderberry blossoms, as well as with apricot, pear or peach wedges.

Tyrolean Ruffles / Tiroler Strauben

- 1 cup milk
- pinch of salt
- 3/4–1 cup flour
- 2 eggs
- 1 T rum or schnapps
- shortening or oil
- 2–3 T sifted powdered sugar

● Slowly heat milk, add salt and stir in sifted flour. let cool slightly, stirring occasionally.

● Fold in egg yolks and the rum or schnapps. Beat the egg whites until stiff and fold in gently.

● Pour batter through funnel or pastry bag to form curls until the size of a plate; fry until evenly brown.

● Sprinkle the warm ruffles with powdered sugar and serve immediately.

F.Y.I.:

"Strauben" are primarily encountered on religious holidays in Tyrol. They are prepared using various batters. This recipe requires that the batter be smooth and easy to pour. "Strauben" can also be made from a milk-cream puff pastry. Regardless of the batter, go heavy on the powdered sugar and serve warm.

Rabbit Ears / Hasenöhrl

(Styria)

2 T butter	1 T rum or schnapps
1/2 cup milk	1 1/4 cups flour
pinch of salt, 1 egg	2 cups shortening or oil

- Melt butter in a skillet; add milk and heat until lukewarm. Add salt and transfer to a mixing bowl. Stir in beaten egg, schnapps or rum and sifted flour.
- Immediately knead into a smooth dough and let stand approx. 1 hour.
- Roll dough out 1/4 inch thick on a floured surface. Cut out diamond-shaped pieces, fold and fry in hot oil.

Honey Ruffles from Ramsau / Ramsauer Perchtstrauben (Styria)

- 1 cup milk
- pinch of salt
- 3/4–1 cup sifted flour
- 2 eggs
- 1 T rum or schnapps
- 2 cups shortening or oil
- 1/2 cup honey

● Heat milk slowly, add salt and stir in sifted flour. let cool slightly, continuing to stir occasionally. Beat egg yolks with rum or schnapps and fold into milk mixture. Beat egg whites until stiff and fold in.

● Heat shortening.

● Pour batter through a funnel or pastry bag to form curls until the size of a plate and fry until brown.

● While the ruffles are still warm, drizzle with honey.

Styrian Snow Balls / Steirische "Schneeballen"

- 1 2/3 cups flour
- pinch of salt
- 1/3 cup sugar
- 1 tsp vanilla extract
- grated rind of 1/2 lemon
- 3–4 T butter
- 3 eggs
- 3–4 T sour cream
- 2 T rum
- 2 cups shortening or oil
- 2–3 T sifted powdered sugar

● Sift flour into a mixing bowl; add salt, sugar, vanilla and lemon zest. Blend in butter and knead to a smooth dough. For best results, use a food processor or electric mixer. Add eggs, sour cream and rum and knead well.

- Form dough into a roll and let stand in a cool place approx. 1 hour.

- Cut roll into 1/3 inch-thick slices. Roll out slices on a floured surface and cut into circles the size of a dessert plate. Use a pastry cutter to evenly trim the circles; make 4 to 5 long incisions in the center of each circle, leaving a 1/2-inch-wide border around the outside. Heat frying oil.

- Using the handle of a wooden spoon, transfer the dough circles to the pan turning slightly.

- Fry until golden, drain well, and serve with a generous dusting of powdered sugar.

Pancakes and Crêpes

Basic Preparation:

Crêpes, known as **"Fluggen"** in Salzburg and as **"Palatschinken"** in the rest of Austria, are prepared from a thin flour batter, which must stand approx. 30 minutes before frying. Whole eggs are used in the batter. However, if lighter crêpes are desired, the batter must be somewhat thick and beaten egg whites folded in. If the crêpes are to be filled, they must be very thin.

"Schmarrn" (sliced pancake), also called **"Tosche"** in Vorarlberg, can be made from a thick batter of flour, bread or baker's cheese. Crêpes are cooked in a large skillet using butter-flavored shortening. Fry until golden on one side, then turn and use two forks to gently pull pancake into bite-size pieces. Complete cooking while turning pieces often. For variation, top with various types of fruit, like apple slices, as is popular in Carinthia.

Cheese Pancake from Montafon / Montafoner "Bolmentosche"

(Vorarlberg)

just over 1 cup baker's cheese
3 egg yolks
1/3 cup sugar
grated rind and juice of 1 lemon
1 cup cream
pinch of salt
3–4 T flour
3 egg whites
4 oz butter or 1/2 cup oil
2–3 T sifted powdered sugar

● Drain baker's cheese well in a sieve and transfer to a mixing bowl. Add egg yolks, half of the sugar, cream, salt and lemon zest and juice. Stir briefly. Sift flour over mixture and mix well. For best results, use an electric mixer.

● Let stand approx. 20 minutes.

● In a separate bowl, beat egg whites until stiff; add remaining sugar gradually, beating well until the mixture is firm. Fold into the cheese mixture.

● Melt half of the butter or shortening in a large skillet and add about half of the cheese mixture. Cook until golden on one side, turn and cook further. Using two forks gently pull pancake into bite-size pieces and continue to cook, turning often. Remove from skillet and keep warm.

● Prepare the rest of the batter in the same fashion.

● Arrange the "Bolmen-tosche" on a warmed plate and dust generously with powdered sugar.

Fan-Shaped Crêpes with strawberries and ice cream / Fächerpalatschinken (Vienna)

Crêpes – see recipe p. 34

fresh strawberries	liqueur
vanilla ice cream	mint leaves

● Fold freshly made crêpes into fan shapes and arrange on dessert plates with several strawberries. Purée strawberries with liqueur and top crêpes as a dessert sauce.

● Lastly, place one scoop of ice cream on each plate and garnish with fresh mint leaves.

Crêpes with Chocolate / Palatschinken mit Schokolade

Crêpes – see recipe p. 34

1/2 cup chocolate shavings	3/4–1 cup whipped cream
	1–2 T sugar

● Spread half of chocolate shavings on fresh crêpes. Roll up and arrange on dessert plates. Top with remaining chocolate shavings and serve with sweet whipped cream.

Crêpes with Nut Filling / Palatschinken mit Nussfülle

Crêpes – see recipe p. 34

1/2 cup ground hazelnuts	pinch of ground cinnamon
3–4 T sugar	6–8 T cream

● Mix ground hazelnuts with sugar and cinnamon; add enough cream to form a creamy mixture. Spread mixture on prepared crêpes, roll up and serve warm.

Cherry Crêpes from the Pongau / "Pongauer Kerschflenggen"

(Salzburg)

just over 1 cup flour	4 egg whites
approx. 1 2/3 cups milk	1 tsp lemon juice
1/4 tsp salt	4 T butter
1–2 T sugar	approx. 10 oz fresh or canned cherries, pitted
4 egg yolks	sugar, optional

● Mix flour, milk, salt and sugar. Add egg yolks stirring after each addition. Let stand approx. 20–30 minutes.

●Beat egg whites with some lemon juice until stiff and fold into egg yolk mixture.

● Melt some butter or shortening in a large skillet. Pour some batter into skillet. Place some cherries on top and fry on both sides. Fry remaining crêpes in the same fashion. If desired, sprinkle with powdered sugar and serve immediately.

Cheese Crêpes / Topfen-Palatschinken

(Vienna)

Basic Recipe:

Batter:

- just over 1 cup flour
- 4 eggs
- approx. 1 2/3 cups milk
- 1/4 tsp salt
- 3 oz butter for frying

Filling:

- 3 T softened butter
- 1/3 cup sugar
- 3 eggs
- 1 1/4 cups baker's cheese
- 1 tsp vanilla extract
- pinch of salt
- grated rind of 1/2 lemon
- 1 T lemon juice
- 1/4 cup raisins

In Addition:

- 3 T sifted powdered sugar

● Mix flour with eggs, milk and salt to form a smooth batter. For best results, use an electric mixer. Let stand approx. 30 minutes.

● For the filling, cream butter with sugar and egg yolks. Fold in drained baker's cheese, vanilla, salt, lemon zest and juice. Beat egg whites until stiff and fold into mixture. Lastly, add rinsed and towel-dried raisins.

● Melt butter in a large skillet. Ladle in about 1/8 of the batter and tip the skillet slightly to cover bottom with batter. Make a

total of 8 "Palatschinken" or crêpes over moderate heat until both sides are golden.

● Spread cheese mixture over each individual crêpe, roll and serve dusted with powdered sugar.

F.Y.I.:

"Palatschinken" (crêpes) have been a staple of Viennese cuisine since the 19th century. These thin pancakes originated in Romania, where they were called "placinta" or "flat cakes." The Hungarians changed the name to "palacinta." When these delicious pancakes arrived in Vienna, they became "Palatschinken."

Emperor's Pancake / Kaiserschmarrn

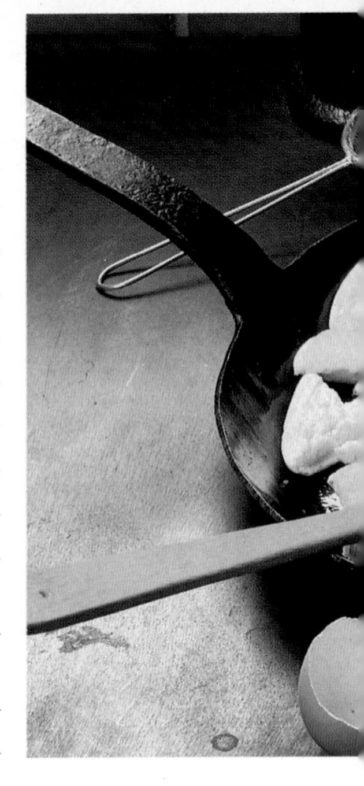

1/4 cup raisins

2–3 T rum

2/3 cup flour, pinch of salt

1 T sifted powdered sugar

1 tsp vanilla extract

grated rind of 1/2 lemon

3 egg yolks, 3 egg whites

1/2 cup milk

1/2 T lemon juice

3 T ground almonds, optional

3/4 T butter **or** margarine for frying

2 T sifted powdered sugar

- Stew raisins and place in a small bowl. Drizzle with rum and set aside. Sift flour into a mixing bowl. Beat in salt, powdered sugar, vanilla, lemon zest, egg yolks and milk. Using an electric mixer or food processor, beat to an easy-to-pour batter and let stand approx. 20–30 minutes.

- Beat egg whites with powdered sugar and a few drops of lemon juice until very stiff. If desired, add ground almonds. Fold egg whites into batter.

- Melt butter in a large skillet. Pour in batter and sprinkle with raisins; cover. Heat until underside is golden brown; turn. Using two

forks, gently pull pancake into bite-sized pieces and complete cooking, turning often. Serve hot, sprinkled generously with powdered sugar.

Our Tip:
Serve "Kaiserschmarrn" with cranberries, apple sauce or a compote. Serve as an entrée or, in smaller portions, as dessert.

F.Y.I.
According to legend, the court chef dedicated this dish to Empress Elizabeth, wife of Austrian Emperor Franz Josef I, calling it the "Empress Pancake" (Kaiserin-Schmarrn). Since it was not to her liking, but instead satisfied the Emperor's sweet tooth, it was simply renamed.

Apple Pancake from Carinthia / Kärntner Apfelschmarrn

just over 1 cup flour

approx. 1 2/3 cups milk

1/4 tsp salt

1–2 T sugar, 4 egg yolks

3 medium apples (approx. 12 oz), 1 T lemon juice

4–5 T butter or margarine for frying

2 T sugar, mixed with 1/2 tsp ground cinnamon

- Mix flour, milk, salt and sugar. For best results, use an electric mixer. Add egg yolks, beating well after each addition. Let stand approx. 10 minutes.
- Meanwhile, peel and core apples; slice into wedges. Place in a mixing bowl and drizzle with lemon juice. Stir to coat.
- Beat egg whites with a few drops of lemon juice until very stiff; fold into batter.
- Melt butter or shortening in a large skillet. Pour in about 1/4 of the batter and arrange apple wedges on top. Fry on both sides.
- Serve whole or sliced, sprinkled with cinnamon sugar.
- Cook remaining batter in the same fashion. Serve warm.

Hot Plum Jam Sandwiches / Liwanzen (Lower Austria)

just over 1 cup flour

1/3 package active dry yeast

2–3 T butter

3–4 T sugar

approx. 1/2 cup milk

1 egg

pinch of salt

oil for frying

butter and plum jam

- Using the ingredients given, prepare a basic yeast dough and let rise.
- Roll dough out approx. 1/4 inch thick on a floured pastry board. Cut out circles approx. 2 1/2 inches in diameter. Let rise.
- Heat oil in a large skillet and fry the dough circles on both sides until golden. Let cool slightly, brush with butter, spread half of the circles with plum jam and sandwich together in twos.

Nockerln or Soufflés
Basic Preparation:

"Salzburger Nockerln," or "Nockerln" for short, are famous well beyond the borders of Salzburg. They are a typical Austrian dessert. "Nockerln" are actually a delicate soufflé made of butter, egg yolks, sugar and beaten egg whites. The recipe, as shown in this book, is not difficult. Well-beaten egg whites are essential to a good "Nockerl" batter. It is just as important that the oven be properly preheated. The baking dish should be large enough and oven-proof. Oval-shaped ovenware,

generously greased, is ideal. "Salzburger Nockerln" belong to the culinary family of soufflés. According to history, this soufflé was first served in the 16th century.

Salzburger Nockerln

- 5 egg whites
- 2 T sugar
- 1 tsp vanilla extract
- 1 tsp lemon juice
- 3 egg yolks
- 2 T flour
- 1 1/2 T softened butter and 1–2 T sugar for the casserole
- 4 T hot milk
- 1 tsp rum
- 2–3 T sifted powdered sugar

● Preheat oven to 400°–425° F.

● Beat egg whites until stiff. Gradually add sugar, vanilla and a few drops of lemon juice until the mixture is very firm.

● Mix egg yolks with flour; fold into egg-white mixture with a few brief strokes.

● Grease an oval casserole dish and sprinkle generously with sugar. Combine hot milk and rum; transfer to dish.

● Gently transfer batter to form 3 large mounds.

Place in oven immediately and bake 14-18 minutes or until golden.

● Serve generously dusted with powdered sugar.

Salzburger Nockerln with Cassis Sauce / Salzburger Nockerln mit Ribisel-Rotweinsosse

Soufflé:

- 2 T softened butter
- 1/2 cup cream
- 1 tsp vanilla extract
- 4 egg yolks
- 1/4 cup sugar
- 2 T dry white wine or rum
- 3 T flour
- pinch of salt
- 8 egg whites
- 1/2 T lemon juice
- 2–3 T sifted powdered sugar

Cassis Sauce:

- 5 T black currant jelly
- 1/2 cup dry red wine
- 1 T honey
- 1 tsp vanilla extract

● Preheat oven to 400°–425° F.

● Boil butter, cream and vanilla in a saucepan. Whisk thoroughly while heating. Set aside.

● Beat egg yolks and sugar until foamy. Add white wine or rum, sifted flour and salt. Stir until creamy.

● Beat egg whites with a few drops of lemon juice until very stiff; fold into batter.

● Transfer the cream sauce and then the egg whites to a large, oven-proof dish. Add the egg whites and use a spatula to form mounds.

● Place in oven immediately and bake approx.

15–20 minutes or until golden.

● Meanwhile prepare the sauce. Boil black currant jelly with red wine, honey and vanilla, stirring well.

● Spoon soufflé onto dessert plates, dust with powdered sugar and drizzle with Cassis sauce. Serve immediately.

Our Tip:
Blackberry jelly may be substituted for black currant jelly, but more sugar should be added. Preparation is the same.

Puddings and Soufflés

Basic Preparation

Puddings can be prepared two different ways. Stove-top puddings call for milk, water, flavorings, fruit and flour, boiled. These require constant stirring so that the mixture does not stick to the bottom of the pan. Always add butter or shortening for flavor.

Other puddings may be steamed in a covered mold. It is important that the mold be only 3/4 full, as the pudding will expand. The water should come to 1/2 inch below the top of the mold.

Soufflés are best baked in a large, oven-proof dish. Only the bottom of the dish needs greasing. After pouring in the batter, smooth the top. For a crustier soufflé, add bread crumbs, sugar or pats of butter on top. Always set the dish on the oven rack in the middle of the oven.

Cheese Pudding / Topfenpudding

(Lower Austria)

- 4–5 T butter
- 1/2 cup sugar
- pinch of salt
- 3 eggs
- just over 2 cups baker's cheese
- 1/3 cup semolina
- 5 T milk
- 1–2 T chopped almonds
- grated rind of 1/2 lemon
- butter and bread crumbs for casserole

● Cream butter with sugar, salt and eggs. Add well-drained baker's cheese, semolina, milk, almonds and lemon zest. Stir well.

● Pour batter into a well-greased pudding mold dusted with white bread crumbs. Set mold in a large double-boiler and steam approx. 60 minutes.

Our Tip:
Applesauce is a good compliment to this dish.

See recipe for "Süesslaschnitz" p. 94.

Bread Pudding from Burgenland / Burgenländer Scheiterhaufen

- 6 slices of dried white bread **or** 6 dried bread rolls
- 2 cups lukewarm milk
- softened butter for casserole
- 3 T softened butter
- 1/3 cup sugar
- 2 T rum
- 4 egg yolks
- grated rind of 1/2 lemon
- 1/4 cup raisins
- 3 T chopped almonds
- 4–5 cooking apples (approx. 1 lb)
- 4 egg whites
- 2 T butter

● Cut rolls into thin slices and place in mixing bowl. Add milk and let stand approx. 30 minutes, stirring occasionally. Preheat oven to 400°–425° F.

● Grease a large casserole dish. Cream butter, sugar, rum and egg yolks. Fold in bread, raisins and almonds.

● Peel, core and slice apples. Fold into batter. Beat egg whites until stiff; gently fold into batter.

● Pour mixture into greased dish and dot with butter. Bake 45–60 minutes or until golden brown.

Our Tip:
Other fruit may be substituted for apples in the same measure. Rhubarb and cherries are recommended. In that case, use roasted hazelnuts rather than chopped almonds.

Moor in a Shirt / “Mohr im Hemd”

(Salzburg)

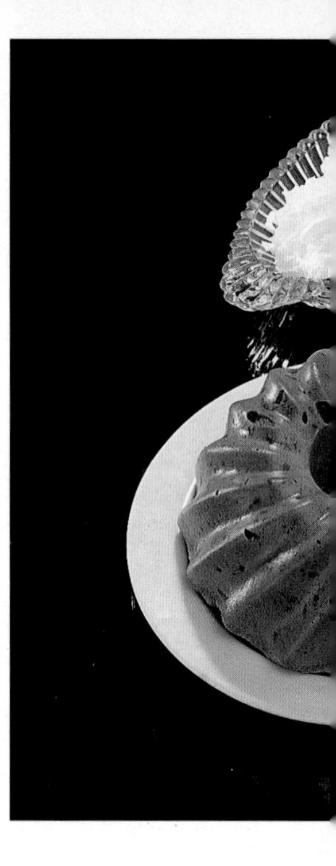

- 4–5 T softened butter
- just over 1/3 cup sugar
- 4 egg yolks
- 4 egg whites
- 1 tsp lemon juice
- 3–4 oz melted dark chocolate
- 2 slices of dried bread **or** 2 dried bread rolls (soaked in milk, squeeze out excess, mill)
- 1/4 cup ground almonds
- 3 T bread crumbs
- softened butter and bread crumbs for the mold
- 1 cup cream
- 2–3 T sugar

● Cream butter, 2/3 of sugar and the egg yolks. Add melted chocolate, bread, ground almonds and bread crumbs. Stir well.

● Beat egg whites until semi-firm; gradually add remaining sugar and a few drops of lemon juice. Beat until very stiff. Gently fold into egg yolk mixture.

● Grease an oven-proof pudding mold and sprinkle with bread crumbs. Pour batter into mold and cover. Set mold in a double-boiler; simmer 1 hour. Let cool, then invert on a platter.

● Serve with sweetened whipped cream.

Our Tip:

If you do not have a mold, you may alternatively use a metal or oven-proof ceramic Bundt pan. Pour the batter into the greased pan dusted with bread crumbs. Set Bundt pan in a deep roasting pan with approx. 1 1/2 qt hot water and cover with a large oven-proof plate. Steam approx. 1 1/2 hours.

Pear Pudding / "Klotzenkoch"

(Salzburg)

2 lb dried pears
water
1 T flour, 2–3 T butter
sugar

● Dice the dried pears and place in a large saucepan. Bring water to a boil and cook pears until soft, stirring occasionally.

● Let cool and put through a meat grinder or purée slightly in a food processor. Blend flour with cold water; add toasted liquid and boil again.

● Arrange on plates and drizzle with melted butter. Dust with sugar and serve warm.

Pudding / Schmalzkoch

(Lower Austria)

just over 1 cup flour
1/2 tsp salt
1–2 eggs
5–7 T cream
3 cups milk
1/2 tsp salt
4 oz butter or shortening for frying
1/2 cup raisins
1/4 cup sugar
1 tsp ground cinnamon, mixed with 1–2 T sugar

● Mix flour, salt, eggs and cream. Knead to form a smooth, semi-firm dough. Let stand 30 minutes. Roll out thinly onto a floured pastry board and cut into small pieces. Separate and let dry somewhat.

● Boil milk, salt and butter-flavored shortening in a large, shallow casserole dish or large skillet.

● Stir in the dough bits, cover and simmer at low temperature approx. 1 hour. Stir occasionally.

● After 30 minutes, fold in the rinsed and towel-dried raisins and sugar. As the end of the cooking time approaches, remove lid. The pudding is finished when all the liquid has been absorbed.

● Serve sprinkled with cinnamon-sugar.

F.Y.I.
This dessert is traditionally served on religious holidays, but is also popular at weddings. It is accompanied by a strong café au lait.

Rice Pudding Trauttmansdorf / Reis Trauttmansdorf

(Vienna)

just over 2 cups milk
just over 1/2 cup long-grain rice
pinch of salt
1 tsp grated lemon rind
12 oz stewed fruits, e.g. cherries, raspberries or pears
3 T sugar
2–3 T rum or maraschino
5 oz gelatin or rice starch
1 cup cream
1–2 T sifted powdered sugar

● Heat milk. Add rice, salt and lemon zest; cook at low temperature approx. 35 minutes. Stir in sugar. Fold in diced fruit marinated in rum or Maraschino with the dissolved gelatin.

● Before the mixture sets, fold in the cream, stiffly beaten with some powdered sugar. Pour mixture into a mold rinsed with cold water and chill.

● To remove from mold, dip briefly into hot water, then invert.

Wine-Laced Bread Pudding / Raabtaler Weinbackerl

(Styria)

- 1/2 cup raisins
- 1/4 cup white wine
- 6–8 slices of dried white bread **or** 6–8 dried bread rolls
- 2 cups warm milk
- 4 T butter
- 4 egg yolks
- 4 T sugar
- 1 tsp vanilla extract
- pinch of salt
- grated rind of 1/2 lemon
- 1/4 cup bread crumbs
- 1/4 cup ground almonds
- 4 egg whites
- 1 tsp lemon juice
- butter and bread crumbs for casserole
- 1/2 cup dry white wine
- 1 T sugar

● Stew raisins and drain; place in a bowl and add wine. Stir to coat and let stand 1 hour, stirring occasionally.

● Pour milk over rolls sliced into thin pieces of the same size. Cream butter, using an electric mixer for best results. Gradually add egg yolks, sugar, vanilla, salt, and lemon zest. Then add raisins, bread crumbs and almonds; mix well.

● Preheat oven to 325°–375° F.

● Beat egg whites with lemon juice until very stiff. Fold into sliced bread mixture. Pour mixture into a greased baking dish dusted with bread crumbs. Bake approx. 35–45 minutes or until golden brown.

● Remove from oven and let cool slightly. Heat wine and sugar; drizzle over bread pudding. Serve immediately.

Apricot Custard / Weicher Marillen-Topfentommerl

(Styria)

- 12 oz fresh or canned apricots
- butter for casserole
- 3 T softened butter
- 1/4 cup sugar
- 2-3 egg yolks
- pinch of salt
- 2/3 cup semolina **or** flour
- 1/2 cup milk
- grated rind of 1/2 lemon
- 1 T lemon juice
- just over 2 cups baker's cheese
- 2–3 egg whites
- 1 T lemon juice

● Halve or quarter apricots and place in a greased, oven-proof dish with cut surface facing up.

● Cream softened butter, sugar, egg yolks and salt in a mixing bowl, using an electric mixer for best results. Stir in wheat semolina or flour, milk, lemon zest and juice. Add well-drained baker's cheese and stir well until smooth.

● Preheat oven to 325°–375° F.

- Beat egg whites with some lemon juice until stiff and fold in.

- Pour batter over the fruit in the dish and smooth over top. Bake approx. 45–55 minutes.

Yeast-Dough Pastries

Basic Preparation:

- Place flour in a mixing bowl and make a well in the center. Crumble yeast into well and pour in some lukewarm milk and 1–2 tsp of the sugar. Stir to form a thick batter. Add some flour; cover this "sponge" and let rise in a warm place approx. 15–20 minutes.
- Add salt, softened butter (shortening or oil), remaining sugar and milk, egg and other flavorings.
- Using dough hooks or the kneading blade of food processor, knead thoroughly until dough is smooth, has a sheen and does not stick to bowl.
- Let rise again approx. 20 minutes. Dough should have noticeably risen and be elastic.

Our Tips

To make sure dough has risen sufficiently, press it with your finger tip; it should bounce back. Always bake yeast dough on a greased, paper-lined baking sheet or in a greased pan.

Tyrolean Nut-Filled Crescent Pastries / Tiroler Nusskipferl

Dough:
- 11 oz butter
- just over 2 cups flour
- 3 T sugar, 4 egg yolks
- 1 package active dry yeast
- 6–7 T lukewarm milk
- pinch of salt
- 1 beaten egg yolk

Filling:
- 3/4 cup ground hazelnuts
- 1/4 cup chopped hazelnuts
- 1 cup sugar
- 1/4 cup milk
- 1 tsp vanilla extract
- 1 T rum, 2 T jam

● Sift flour into a bowl and dot with butter. Add sugar, egg yolks and yeast dissolved in lukewarm milk as well as salt; knead until smooth. Turn dough out on to a floured surface and roll until very thin; cut into squares.

● Preheat oven to 400°–425°F. Mix all ingredients for the filling and distribute on dough squares. Form squares into crescents and brush with egg yolk. Place on a greased baking sheet dusted with flour and bake 15–20 minutes or until golden brown.

Filled Doughnuts / Feine “Krapfa”

just over 2 cups flour	2–3 egg yolks
1 package active dry yeast	3–4 oz softened butter
1/3 cup sugar	just over 2 cups shortening **or** oil
1 tsp vanilla extract	4 T apricot jam
pinch of salt	2–3 T sifted powdered sugar
approx. 1 cup lukewarm milk	

- Sift flour into a large mixing bowl and make a well in the center. Crumble in yeast and stir in some milk and sugar to make a “sponge.” Cover and let rise approx. 20–30 minutes in a warm place.

- Add the remaining milk, sugar, vanilla, salt, egg yolks and softened butter; knead to a smooth dough that does not stick to bowl. For best results, use a food processor or electric mixer.

- Turn dough onto a floured surface and roll out until approx. 3/4 inch thick. Using a glass, cut out circles approx. 3 inches in diameter. Cover with a dry towel and let rise approx. 15–20 minutes.

- Heat shortening for frying and gently drop in dough circles to fry approx. 3 minutes on each side or until golden brown. Turn at least once.

- Carefully remove doughnuts using a slotted spoon and drain on paper towels.

- Once cool, fill with apricot marmalade if desired. For best results, use a pastry tube. Serve with a generous dusting of powdered sugar.

Fruit Coffee Ring / Vorarlberger Ofenkatze (Vorarlberg)

just over 2 cups flour
1 package active dry yeast
1/4–1/3 cup sugar
1 tsp vanilla extract
pinch of salt
approx. 1 cup lukewarm milk
2 eggs
4 oz softened butter
2 T dried pears
1/2 cup raisins
1 T rum
1 T sugar
1/4 tsp ground cinnamon
1 T butter for the pan
1 T bread crumbs

● Sift flour into a large bowl. Make a well in the center; crumble in yeast and stir in some milk and sugar to make a "sponge." Cover and let rise approx. 20–30 minutes in a warm place.

● Add the remaining milk, sugar, vanilla, salt, eggs and softened butter to yeast mixture. Mix diced pears and raisins with rum. Sprinkle with sugar and cinnamon and let stand. Add this mixture to the yeast dough and knead thoroughly until dough does not stick to bowl. For best results, use a food processor or electric mixer.

● Let rise again 15–20 minutes. Turn out onto a floured surface. Set in a greased Bundt pan dusted with bread crumbs.

● Let rise another 10–15 minutes, then bake in oven preheated to 325°–350° F for 50–60 minutes.

● Let cool slightly in pan. Loosen sides and invert.

Tyrolean Easter Coffee Ring / Tiroler Oster-Fochaz

Dough:

just over 4 cups flour

1 package active dry yeast

1/3 cup sugar

approx. 1 cup lukewarm milk

3 egg yolks

1/2 tsp salt

1/2 cup melted butter

Glaze:

1 egg yolk, 2 T milk

● Sift flour into a large bowl. Make a well in the center; crumble in yeast and stir in some milk and sugar. Cover and let rise approx. 20–30 minutes in a warm place.

● Add the remaining milk, egg yolks, salt and butter to yeast mixture. Knead thoroughly to a smooth dough that does not stick to bowl. Let rise 15–20 minutes longer.

● Preheat oven to 350°–400° F. Divide dough into 3 equal portions. Roll each portion into an 18-inch rope. Braid the 3 ropes and join the ends to form a wreath. Place on a greased baking sheet and let rise again. Brush with beaten egg yolk and bake 40–50 minutes or until golden brown.

Plum Jam Kolatchen / Powidl-Kolatschen (Lower Austria)

just over 2 cups flour
1 package active dry yeast
3 1/2 oz softened butter
1/3 cup sugar
approx. 1 cup milk
1 tsp vanilla extract
3 egg yolks
grated rind of 1/2 lemon
plum jam or marmalade
1–2 beaten eggs, some water

● Prepare basic yeast dough (p. 58) with ingredients given and let rise.

● Roll dough 1/4 inch thick and cut into squares approx. 5x5 inches. Place 1 T of the filling in the center of each square and brush the corners with a mixture of beaten egg and a few drops of water. Fold edges in to the center. Place on a greased baking sheet and let rise again. Meanwhile, preheat oven to 350°–400° F.

● Brush the risen kolatchen with egg again and bake 30–35 minutes.

Plum Jam Doughnuts / Germkrapfen mit Zwetschgenfülle (Carinthia)

just over 2 cups flour
1 package active dry yeast
1/3 cup sugar
1 tsp vanilla extract
pinch of salt
approx. 1 cup lukewarm milk
2–3 egg yolks
4 oz softened butter
just over 2 cups shortening **or** oil
4–5 T plum jam
2–3 T sifted powdered sugar

● Sift flour into a large mixing bowl and make a well in the center. Crumble in yeast and stir in some

milk and sugar. Cover and let rise approx. 20–30 minutes in a warm place.

● Add the remaining milk, sugar, vanilla, salt, egg yolks and softened butter; knead to a smooth dough that does not stick to bowl. For best results, use a food processor or electric mixer.

● Turn dough onto a floured surface and roll out until approx. 3/4 inch thick. Using a glass, cut out circles approx. 3 inches in diameter. Cover with a dry towel and let rise approx. 15–20 minutes.

● Heat shortening for frying and gently drop in dough circles to fry approx. 3 minutes on each side or until golden brown. Turn at least once.

● Remove doughnuts carefully using a slotted spoon and drain on paper towels.

● Once cool, fill with plum marmalade if desired. For best results, use a pastry tube. Serve with a dusting of powdered sugar.

Carinthian Cinnamon Buns / Kärntner Reindling

Dough:

- just over 2 cups flour
- 1 package active dry yeast
- 1/3 cup sugar
- 1 tsp vanilla extract
- pinch of salt
- approx. 1 cup milk
- 2–3 eggs
- 4 oz softened butter

Filling:

- 2 oz softened butter
- 1/2 cup sugar
- 1 T ground cinnamon
- 1/2 cup raisins
- 2 oz butter for pan

● Sift flour into a large mixing bowl and make a well in the center. Crumble in yeast and stir in some milk and sugar to make a "sponge." Cover and let rise approx. 20–30 minutes in a warm place.

● Add the remaining milk, sugar, vanilla, salt, eggs and softened butter; knead to a smooth dough that does not stick to bowl. For best results, use a food processor or electric mixer.

● Turn dough onto a floured surface and roll out until approx. 3/4 inch thick and cover with a dry towel.

● Melt butter and brush on dough. Mix sugar and cinnamon and sprinkle over dough. Rinse and dry raisins using paper towels; sprinkle over dough.

● Roll dough jelly-roll fashion and place on a well-greased enamel baking sheet or better yet in a greased Bundt pan.

● Let rise another 15–20 minutes, then bake 50–60 minutes in an oven preheated to 325°–350° F.

● Cool slightly in the pan. Loosen sides and invert.

Viennese Sweet Buns / Buchteln (Wuchteln) Wiener Art

- just over 2 cups flour
- pinch of salt
- 1 package active dry yeast
- approx. 1/4 cup lukewarm milk
- 1 egg
- 1/3 cup sugar
- 1 tsp vanilla extract
- 3 oz softened butter
- grated rind of 1/2 lemon
- 3 1/2 oz butter
- 3–4 T apricot or plum jam

● Sift flour into a large mixing bowl and make a well in the center. Crumble in yeast and stir in some milk and sugar. Cover and let rise approx. 20–30 minutes in a warm place.

● Add the remaining milk, sugar, vanilla, salt, egg butter and lemon zest; knead to a smooth dough that does not stick to bowl.

● Turn dough onto a floured surface and roll out until approx. 3/4 inch thick. Cut out squares; spread 1 tsp of marmalade or plum sauce on each and roll together.

● Grease a large enamel or oven-proof casserole dish and arrange buns next to each other, smooth side up. Cover and let rise 15–20 minutes. Preheat oven to 350°–400° F.

● Brush tops of buns generously with butter. Place in oven and bake approx. 45 minutes brushing with butter again.

● The buns are ready when the tops are golden.

Our Tip:
Serve with vanilla sauce.

Dried Brioche / Grazer Triëtschnitten (Styria)

Dough:

- 1 1/2 cups flour
- 1/2 package active dry yeast
- 2 T sugar
- 2 T softened butter
- 1/2 cup lukewarm milk
- 1 egg, pinch of salt

Dredging Mixture:

- 1/4 cup sugar
- 1/2 tsp ground cinnamon

Sauce:

- 2 cups dry white wine
- 1/2 tsp ground cinnamon
- some ground cloves
- grated rind of 1/2 lemon, 2–3 T sugar

● Prepare basic yeast dough (recipe p. 58) with the ingredients given and let rise.

● Meanwhile preheat oven to 325°–350° F.

● Place dough in a rectangular baking dish and bake 30–45 minutes or until golden brown.

● While still warm, cut into approx. 3/4-inch-thick slices and place on a greased baking sheet. Let dry in the oven at 250°–300° F. Dredge in a cinnamon-sugar mixture.

● Make a mulled wine from wine, cinnamon, nutmeg, lemon zest and sugar.

● Arrange slices on plates and pour wine sauce over them. Let buns absorb sauce; serve warm.

F.Y.I.

The drying of the "Triët" in the hot oven is called "bähen".

Rich Egg Pastry

Basic Preparation:

- Sift flour and baking powder into a mixing bowl. Add sugar, eggs, spices, slices of butter or margarine and other ingredients, depending upon the recipe.

- To prevent flour from dusting the kitchen, start dough hooks at the lowest setting, then turn up to the highest setting for 2 minutes to form a ball. If the dough is crumbly, add some liquid or knead briefly by hand.

- Wrap in plastic wrap and chill for 30 minutes.

Our Tips:

Only small amounts (1 pinch per 8-10 oz flour) of baking powder are needed. Sugar should always be fine-grained. The rule is one part sugar to four parts flour.

A rich egg pastry with more sugar browns better. Egg yolks make the dough more tender, egg whites make it crispier. Vanilla, lemon zest and a pinch of salt complete the taste of every sweet, rich pastry dough. The bottom of the dough is pricked several times with a fork to prevent air bubbles in the dough while baking. When baking crusts with high edges, we recommend cooking the pastry shell alone first. The pastry shell is placed in the dish and covered with a paper lining. Fill the pastry shell up to the edges with beans, peas, etc. These are then removed after the shell has been baked.

After baking, rich egg pastries should be removed from the baking sheet or dish immediately to prevent sticking. Always let rich egg pastries cool on a wire rack. With cookies, it is best to let them cool on a cookie sheet lined with paper.

Classic Vanilla Stars from Salzburg / Vanillesterne Alt-Salzburger Art

5 oz butter, 2/3 cup sugar	just over 1 cup flour
2 egg yolks	1 beaten egg yolk
2 tsp vanilla extract	decorative sugar
2 T rum, pinch of salt	

- Blend ingredients given to a fine pastry dough. Chill approx. 15 minutes.
- Roll to 1/4-inch thickness and cut out stars of different sizes. Chill again, then brush with beaten egg yolk. Sprinkle with decorative sugar. Place on a greased or lined baking sheet.
- Bake at 350°–400° F in a preheated oven for 12–16 minutes or until golden.

Makes approx. 80 cookies

Chocolate-Covered Jam Cookies / Ischler Gebäck (Upper Austria)

1 1/4 cups flour
2/3 cup sugar
2/3 cup ground almonds
pinch of salt
pinch of ground cinammon
1 T rum
10 oz butter
red-colored marmalade
3–4 T melted chocolate
chopped pistachios, chopped almonds **or** 2–3 T sifted powdered sugar

● Sift flour into a mixing bowl and make a well in the center. Add sugar, almonds, spices and rum. Add butter cut in slices. Working from the center, knead to a smooth dough.
● Roll dough to approx. 1/8-inch thickness, cut out circles and place on a greased or lined baking sheet. Bake at 325°–350° F in a preheated oven for 12–18 minutes.
● After cooling, make jam sandwiches with two cookies each and drizzle with chocolate. Garnish as desired.
Makes approx. 45 cookies

Little Vanilla Crescent Cookies / Wiener Vanillekipferl (Vienna)

1 1/4 cups flour
1/2 cup sugar
1 tsp vanilla extract
3 egg yolks
1/2 cup ground almonds
9 oz butter
3 T vanilla sugar

● Work all ingredients to a smooth dough and chill approx. 1 hour.

● Form dough into a thin roll; cut even slices and form into little crescents. Place on a well-greased or lined baking sheet.

● Bake at 325°–375° F in a preheated oven for 12–16 minutes or until golden. Dredge in vanilla sugar while still hot.

Makes approx. 60 cookies

Linzer Torte

(Upper Austria)

- 2/3 cup flour
- 2/3 cup ground almonds
- 2/3 cup sugar
- 1 tsp vanilla extract
- pinch of salt
- 1 tsp ground cinammon
- pinch of ground cloves
- grated rind of 1 lemon
- 4 egg yolks
- 5 oz softened butter
- 3/4 cup black currant jam
- 1/4 cup almond slivers
- butter and bread crumbs or ground almonds for the pan
- 1 T sifted powdered sugar

● Sift flour into a mixing bowl. Add almonds, sugar, vanilla, salt, cinnamon, ground cloves and lemon zest; stir well. Add 3 egg yolks and butter, chilled and sliced. Using a food processor or electric mixer, work to form a smooth dough. Cover and chill approx. 30 minutes.

● Preheat oven to 340°–375° F. Grease a dark-colored 9-inch spring form pan and sprinkle with bread crumbs if desired. Distribute 2/3 of the dough evenly in pan. Brush dough with black currant jam, leaving a 1/2-inch edge free. Roll half of remaining dough into thin strips. Weave a lattice over the jam. Use remaining dough to form a good edge around torte. Brush with remaining egg yolk and sprinkle with shaved almond slivers. Bake 40–50 minutes or until golden brown. Let cool and serve with a generous dusting of powdered sugar.

Our Tip:
Linzer Tortes can be prepared well in advance. Simply wrap in aluminum foil to store, and it will taste oven-fresh even after a few days.

Apple Torte from Fürstenfeld / Fürstenfelder Apfeltorte (Styria)

Crust:
- just over 1 cup flour
- 4 oz butter
- 1/4 cup sugar
- 1 egg

Filling:
- 3 egg yolks
- 2/3 cup sugar
- 1 tsp vanilla extract
- pinch of salt
- 1 T lemon juice
- 1 T rum
- 1 baking apple
- 3 egg whites
- 1 tsp lemon juice
- 3/4 cup ground almonds
- 2 T flour
- 1/2 tsp baking powder
- 6 small baking apples (approx. 1 1/4 lb)
- 3 T melted butter and 2–3 T red-colored marmalade
- 2–3 T sifted powdered sugar

● Work flour, butter, sugar and egg to a pastry dough. Chill approx. 30 minutes.

● Preheat oven to 340°–375° F.

● Distribute 2/3 of the dough evenly in a 9-inch spring form pan. Form remaining dough into a roll and place along the pastry edge, using your hands to work dough 1 inch high on the pan's sides. Prick pastry several times with a fork.

● Bake approx. 15 minutes in hot oven.

● Meanwhile, beat egg yolks, sugar, vanilla and salt until frothy. For best results, use an electric mixer. Add lemon juice and rum; stir. Peel and grate one apple; add to batter. Beat egg whites with lemon juice until stiff and fold into batter. Sift flour with baking powder; mix with ground almonds and add to batter, stirring well. Distribute batter evenly in baked pastry shell.

● Peel, core and cut apples in half. On the rounded side of the apples make several vertical incisions; arrange apples on top of the almond batter.

● Bake 50–60 minutes. Brush with melted butter after 25–30 minutes. Remove from oven, remove torte from pan and glaze with rose-hip jam. Let cool. Dust with powdered sugar and serve.

Spongecakes and Meringues

Basic Preparation

Variation 1 (eggs separated)

Beat egg whites, with or without cold water, and vanilla. Gradually sprinkle in sugar by the spoonful, beating well. Fold in beaten egg yolks and other flavorings. In a separate bowl mix sifted flour with baking powder, cornstarch or cocoa, whichever applies. Sift into batter and fold.

Variation 2 (whole eggs)

Beat whole eggs, with or without warm water, until foamy. For best results, use a food processor or electric mixer. Gradually add sugar and other flavorings, mixing at highest speed. Mix until creamy and glossy. Mix sifted flour with baking powder, cornstarch or possibly cocoa. Sift into batter and fold.

Our Tips:
Only the freshest eggs will become light and airy with beating, giving the batter volume. The sugar should be fine-grained, so that it dissolves quickly. For tortes, up to 1/3 of flour can be substituted by cornstarch. It is easiest to line the bottom of the pan or baking sheet. Never grease the sides of the pan as the melted butter may drip into the batter. Bake the mixed spongecake batter immediately or it will deflate.

Using Egg Whites:
When making pastries and desserts, you may have egg whites left over because egg yolks are more frequently called for. Egg whites may be stored in the refrigerator in a tightly sealed jar for several days and remain fresh and easy to beat.

There are several recipes in which only egg whites or beaten egg whites are used instead of whole eggs.

These include:
- all types of macaroons
- meringues
- Salzburger Nockerln
- egg-white glazes

Various Fillings and Glazes

Buttercream

9 oz softened butter
1 cup sifted powdered sugar
pinch of salt
2 fresh egg yolks
flavoring

Whip softened butter until creamy; gradually add powdered sugar and lastly salt, egg yolks and flavorings, such as:

- **vanilla** from vanilla bean or vanilla extract
- 1 tsp **lemon zest** and 2–3 T lemon juice
- 1 tsp grated **orange peel** and 3–4 T orange juice
- 2–3 T **mocha** and 1 T brandy
- 1–2 T **cocoa** and/or 1–2 T **chocolate shavings**
- 2–3 T **rum**
- 3 1/2 oz ground **hazelnuts or walnuts** and 1–1 1/2 T rum

Our Tip:

Buttercream will stay firm if you add approx. 3/4 oz shortening (coconut fat).

Coconut Macaroons / Kokosbusserl (Lower Austria)

- 4 egg whites
- just over 1 cup sugar
- 1 tsp vanilla extract
- pinch of salt
- 1–2 tsp lemon juice
- 1–1 1/4 cups shredded coconut
- baking wafers
- 1/4 cup melted chocolate

● Beat egg whites until very stiff. Gradually sprinkle in sugar by the spoonful, and vanilla. Add salt and lemon juice and beat until very firm and glossy. Fold in shredded coconut.

● Preheat oven to 250°-275° F. Using two spoons, scoop mounds of batter onto wafers and place approx. 3/4 inch apart on baking sheet.

● Bake 35–40 minutes. Macaroons should be almost white outside, and still soft inside. Melt chocolate coating, cool and fill in a pastry bag or plastic bag with a corner cut off. Artfully drizzle coating over macaroons. Once cool, cut away any protruding wafer.

Makes approx. 35–40 cookies

Rum-Almond Cookies / Muskazonerl (Tyrol)

- 2/3 cup sugar
- 2 egg yolks
- 1 tsp lemon juice
- 2/3 cup ground almonds
- 2 T bread crumbs
- 1–2 T rum
- baking wafers

● Mix sugar and egg yolks in a deep mixing bowl. Use an electric mixer for best results. Add lemon juice, ground almonds and rum-soaked bread crumbs; stir.

● Preheat oven to 275°–325° F. Line cookie sheet. Arrange wafers on sheet and place approx. 2 tsp of batter on each. Bake 15–20 minutes.

Makes approx. 20–25 cookies

Anise Cookies / Anislaibl

4 eggs
1 cup sifted powdered sugar
1 tsp ground anise
1 1/4 cups flour
butter to grease the cookie sheet

- Grease baking sheet and dust with flour. Tap sheet to remove excess flour.
- Preheat oven to 275°–325° F.
- Cream eggs and sugar in a deep mixing bowl. Add anise. Stir in sifted flour gradually so that the batter is smooth, not too stiff.
- Using two teaspoons, scoop mounds of batter onto baking sheet, placing approx. 1 inch apart.
- Bake approx. 15–18 minutes or until golden.

Makes approx. 40

Hazelnut Torte / Oberösterreichische Nusstorte (Upper Austria)

Nut Batter:
7 eggs
5 T warm water
1 1/4 cups sugar
2 T rum
just over 1 cup ground hazelnuts
2/3 cup flour
1 tsp baking powder
4 T lemon juice, mixed with 4 T rum

Filling:
buttercream, see p. 75

Garnish:
1/4 cup ground hazelnuts
16 whole hazelnuts

- Preheat oven to 325°–350° F. Line a 9-inch spring form pan.
- Using the ingredients given, make basic spongecake batter (see p. 74). Pour batter into pan.
- Bake 50–65 minutes. Remove from pan; invert on a wire rack and let cool.

- Cut through the torte twice horizontally and drench with lemon-rum mixture.
- Spread buttercream on each layer and reassemble. Frost the top and sides. Decorate edge with ground nuts. Using a pastry bag, decorate top of cake with 16 frosting dots and affix one whole hazelnut on each dot.
- Let cool thoroughly.

Mozart Torte / Salzburger Mozarttorte (Salzburg)

Batter:
4 egg yolks
3/4 cup sugar
4 T warm water
1 tsp vanilla extract
4 egg whites
1/2 cup flour
1/2 cup cornstarch
2 T cocoa powder
3 tsp baking powder

Filling:
4 oz softened butter
2/3 cup sifted powdered sugar
1/2 cup cocoa powder
2 T water
1 egg
some rum
1 tsp vanilla extract
7 oz marzipan
approx. 1 1/2 cups apricot jam

Garnish:
bonbons for decoration

- Preheat oven to 340°–375° F.
- Beat egg yolks with water; gradually add sugar and vanilla, stirring well after each addition to form a creamy mixture. Beat egg whites until stiff and fold into cream mixture. Combine flour, cornstarch, cocoa and baking powder; sift, folding into cream mixture. Grease bottom of a 10-inch, round cake pan; line pan with parchment or baking paper and pour in batter.
- Bake 25–35 minutes. Let cool slightly in pan. Invert on a wire rack and wet paper to carefully remove lining.

- For the filling, beat softened butter; add mixture of powdered sugar and cocoa gradually. Add egg, rum, water and vanilla, stirring until creamy.
- Cut through the torte twice horizontally. Divide marzipan into two pieces, knead until supple and roll each to size of cake. Brush layers with chocolate cream and top with marzipan. Top this with apricot jam and stack layers. Press lightly and frost top and sides with remaining chocolate cream. Decorate with bonbons and chill at least 2 hours.

Cakes

Basic Preparation:

- Sift mixture of flour and/or cornstarch as well as baking powder or cocoa into a deep mixing bowl.
- Add sugar, vanilla, salt, softened butter or margarine, and possibly lemon zest, eggs, milk, and rum.
- To prevent flour from dusting the kitchen, start electric mixer at lowest setting, then beat at highest setting.
- Lastly, depending upon recipe, stir in other ingredients like raisins, ground nuts, candied lemon or orange peel, chocolate shavings or drained fruit. Mixing time: approx. 2–3 minutes.

Our Tips:

Cakes should always bake in a pan greased and dusted with bread crumbs or lined. Dark-colored pans are better than stainless steel, because they conduct the heat better. The pan should

always be large enough and should only be filled two-thirds of the way, so the batter does not spill over. Let cake cool slightly in pan for a few minutes; then invert onto a wire rack.

Raisin Coffee Cake / Kärntner Weinbeerl-Guglhupf (Carinthia)

- 9 oz softened butter
- 1 cup sugar
- 1 tsp vanilla extract
- pinch of salt
- 4 eggs
- 1 1/4 cups flour
- 1/2 cup cornstarch
- 2 tsp baking powder
- 4 T rum
- approx. 1/2 cup milk
- 1/3 cup raisins
- 1/4 cup ground almonds
- grated rind of 1 lemon
- pinch of ground cinammon
- butter and bread crumbs for the pan
- 2 T sifted powdered sugar

● Cream softened butter, sugar, vanilla, salt and eggs in that order. Use an electric mixer for best results. Combine flour, cornstarch and baking powder; sift over cream mixture and stir. Add rum, milk, rinsed and towel-dried raisins, almonds, lemon zest and cinnamon.

● Grease a Bundt pan and dust with bread crumbs.

● Preheat oven to 340°–375° F.

● Pour batter into pan and smooth top. Bake 60–70 minutes.

● Let cool slightly in pan, loosen sides from pan and invert on a wire rack to cool. Generously dust with powdered sugar and serve.

Viennese Walnut-Apple Torte / Wiener Walnuss-Apfeltorte

Batter:
3 1/2 oz softened butter
1/2 cup sugar
1 tsp vanilla extract
2 eggs
2/3 cup flour
1 tsp ground cinnamon
2–3 T rum
3 medium baking apples
Egg-White Mixture:
4 egg whites
pinch of salt
1 cup sifted powdered sugar
1 tsp lemon juice
1 cup ground walnuts
2 tsp ground cinnamon
2 T amaretto liqueur
Garnish:
3 gelatin envelopes
1 1/2 cups cream
pinch of ground cinnamon
sugarpearls
bread crumbs, butter for the pan
1 piece of aluminum foil

● Prepare batter as described on p. 80.

● Pour batter into a greased, 8-inch spring form pan dusted with bread crumbs.

● Peel, quarter and core apples; slice and arrange on batter.

● Beat egg whites with salt and lemon juice until very stiff. Gradually beat in powdered sugar until the mixture is glossy and firm. Gently fold in ground walnuts, cinnamon and liqueur.

● Top apples in pan with egg-white mixture and cover with aluminum foil. Bake approx. 35–40 minutes at 340°-375° F. Remove foil and bake another 15–25 minutes until the top is crispy and light brown.

● Remove torte from pan and cool. To decorate, dissolve gelatin in cold water approx. 10 minutes. Whip cream. Add the cool,

liquid gelatin to the whipped cream, stirring constantly. Let cool.

- Frost torte with cream, forming waves. Cool further. Sprinkle with cinnamon and festive silver pearls before serving.

Makes 16 pieces

Innsbruck Fruit Cake / Innsbrucker Früchtekuchen (Tyrol)

- 1/4 cup sultanas, 1 T rum
- 1/4 cup candied lemon peel
- 1/4 cup candied orange peel, 7 oz butter
- 1 1/4 cups flour, pinch of salt
- 1 cup sugar, 6 eggs
- 1 tsp vanilla extract
- grated rind of 1/2 lemon
- 3 T rum
- 1 tsp baking powder
- butter and bread crumbs for pan

● Rinse, drain and pat dry sultanas; drizzle with rum and let stand approx. 1 hour.

● Dice candied lemon and orange peel.

● Cream butter and sugar; add eggs, stirring constantly. Stir in vanilla, lemon zest and rum a few drops at a time. Add flour sifted with baking powder and salt, sultanas and candied lemon and orange peels. Mix until smooth.

● Grease a 10-inch-long loaf pan and dust with bread crumbs. Pour in batter and bake 55-65 minutes in a preheated oven at 340°–375° F.

Our Tip:
Thoroughly cooled and wrapped in aluminum foil, this cake will still taste oven-fresh even after a few days.

Almond Coffee Cake / Feiner Mandelguglhupf (Salzburg)

- 9 oz softened butter
- 1 cup sugar
- 1 tsp vanilla extract
- 4 eggs
- 1 1/4 cups flour
- 1/2 cup cornstarch
- 2 tsp baking powder
- 4 T rum
- approx. 1/2 cup milk
- 1/2 cup chopped almonds
- 3–4 drops almond aroma
- 2–3 T sifted powdered sugar
- butter and bread crumbs for pan

● Cream butter, sugar, vanilla and eggs in that order. Use an electric mixer for best results. Combine flour with cornstarch and baking powder; sift into cream mixture and stir.

● Then stir in rum, milk and almonds.

● Grease and dust a Bundt pan with bread crumbs. Pour in batter and bake 60–75 minutes in a preheated oven at 340°–375° F.

● Let cool briefly in pan. Loosen cake from pan and invert on a wire rack. Cool. Serve generously dusted with powdered sugar.

Tyrolean Poppy-Seed Coffee Cake / Tiroler Mohnguglhupf

- 9 oz softened butter
- 1 cup sugar
- pinch of salt
- 1 tsp vanilla extract
- 4 eggs
- 1 1/4 cups flour
- 1/2 cup cornstarch
- 2 tsp baking powder
- 3 T rum
- approx. 1/2 cup milk
- 1/4 cup chopped almonds
- 1/2–3/4 cup ground poppy seeds
- 2–3 T sifted powdered sugar
- butter and bread crumbs for pan

● Grease and dust a Bundt pan with bread crumbs. Preheat oven to 340°–375° F.

● Cream butter with sugar, salt, vanilla and eggs, in that order. Sift in flour mixed with cornstarch and baking powder; stir well. Then stir in rum, milk, ground almonds and poppy seeds. Pour batter into pan and bake 60–70 minutes.

● Let cool briefly in pan. Invert and serve cooled with a generous dusting of powdered sugar.

Sachertorte / Wiener Sachertorte
(Vienna)

- 5 oz butter
- 1/2 cup sifted powdered sugar
- 8 egg yolks
- 2/3 cup dark chocolate
- 2/3 cup flour
- 8 egg whites
- 1/4 cup sugar
- 2 T apricot jam
- 1 cup cream
- 1/2 cup dark chocolate glaze

● Cream softened butter and powdered sugar. Beat in egg yolks individually and mix until creamy using an electric mixer or food processor. Melt chocolate bits in a double boiler or in the microwave. Stir until lukewarm, then stir into cream by the teaspoonful. Sift in flour. Beat egg whites with sugar until stiff; fold in with a whisk.

● Line the bottom of a 9-inch spring form pan. Pour in batter. Bake approx. 50–65 minutes at 340°–375° F. Remove and let cool. Remove torte from pan and let cool thoroughly on a wire rack. Remove lining and, if necessary, even out cake bottom with a knife.

● Heat apricot preserves while stirring. Smooth over

entire torte, including sides.

● Melt commercial chocolate glaze and frost cake. Decorate if desired. Serve with whipped cream.

F.Y.I.

This recipe, though typical, is not the one for the "Original Sachertorte", which is a heavily guarded secret of the Hotel Sacher in Vienna. In the peak season, over 4000 tasty tortes are produced each day by the Hotel Sacher, ready to export to all corners of the world.

Cheese Stollen / Topfenstollen
(Upper Austria)

Dough:
- 1 1/4 cups baker's cheese
- 5 oz softened butter
- 2/3 cup sugar
- 1 tsp vanilla extract
- 1/4 tsp salt
- grated rind of 1 lemon
- 1/4 tsp ground cinnamon
- 1 egg, 1 1/2 cups flour
- 1/2 cup cornstarch
- 2 tsp baking powder
- 1/2 cup almond slivers
- 1 cup dried mixed fruits
- 2 T rum
- melted butter
- 2–3 T sifted powdered sugar

- Combine baker's cheese, softened butter, sugar, vanilla, salt, lemon zest, cinnamon, egg, flour, cornstarch and baking powder in a mixing bowl. Using a hand-held electric mixer, knead to a smooth dough. Then add almond slivers and rum mixed with diced, dried fruit. Knead well again.
- Roll onto a floured surface and fold 1/3 over to make the classic stollen shape. Place on a well-greased and floured (or lined) baking sheet. Bake 50–65 minutes in a preheated oven at 350°–400° F.
- While still hot, brush with melted butter and dust generously with powdered sugar.

Creams and Sweet Sauces

Basic Preparation:

Creams:

These delicious desserts are made from a basic liquid, namely milk, fruit juice or wine, and a frothy mixture of eggs and sugar. Stirred creams are bound with gelatin dissolved in cream. For whipped creams, soak the gelatin, squeeze out the excess liquid and then dissolve the gelatin in hot liquid.

Sweet Sauces:

Cream sauces are made by boiling milk or wine with sugar and eggs and sometimes thickened with cornstarch. With the addition of flavorings, this basic mixture becomes a vanilla, chocolate or caramel sauce.

Fruit Sauces:

These are made with fresh, puréed fruits or compotes, depending on the season. To thin, use fruit juices or wine. Both go well with cold and warm desserts.

Raspberry Cream / Himbeercreme
(Upper Austria)

1 1/2 lb fresh or frozen raspberries, thawed
2 tsp vanilla extract
sugar as needed
2 envelopes of white gelatin
2 envelopes of red gelatin
2 cups cream

- Rinse berries, remove stems and purée, setting some aside for garnish. Sweeten with vanilla and sugar to taste.
- Dissolve gelatin and add, stirring rapidly; chill.
- If the cream is too thick, whip cream and fold in half.
- Pour into a mold rinsed with cold water and chill.
- Invert to serve and garnish with whipped cream and fruit.

Rum-Chocolate Cream / Rum-Schokoladencreme

2/3 cup chocolate
5 oz softened butter
2 tsp vanilla extract
pinch of salt
4 egg yolks
4 T rum

- Melt chocolate in a double-boiler and cool. Cream butter with vanilla and salt. Stir in egg yolks and chocolate alternately. Mix until smooth and flavor with rum.

Weinschaum Sauce / Weinchaudeau
(Vienna)

3 egg yolks
1/2 cup sugar
1 1/4 T cornstarch
2 cups dry white wine
grated rind and juice of 1/2 lemon

● Beat egg yolks and sugar until frothy; add cornstarch, wine and lemon juice and zest.

● Whisk constantly in a double-boiler or over mild heat until the mixture is thick and frothy (do not boil). Serve warm or cold.

Viennese Mocha Cream / Wiener Mokkacreme

2 egg yolks

2–3 tsp instant coffee powder

2 cups milk

1/4 cup sugar

1 tsp vanilla extract

1 envelope white gelatin

2 egg whites

1/2 cup cream

2–3 T grated dark chocolate

● Mix egg yolks and instant coffee with some milk. Gradually bring remaining milk to a boil with sugar, salt and vanilla; remove from heat. Stir in egg yolk-coffee mixture and the gelatin dissolved according to package. Chill.

● As soon as the mixture thickens, fold in stiffly beaten egg whites and cream.

● Pour into serving dishes and once set, garnish with grated chocolate.

Apricot Sauce / Marillensosse

(Burgenland)

1 lb fresh, ripe apricots

1 cup water or white wine

1/2 cup sugar

juice of 1 lemon

pinch of ground ginger

1–2 T rum or apricot liquer

● Remove pits from apricots and stew in water or wine; put through a food mill.

● Mix apricots with sugar and lemon juice; thin with cooking liquid if necessary. Add ginger and rum or apricot liqueur to taste.

Raspberry Jelly Roll / Himbeer-Biskuitroulade (Burgenland)

Batter:	Filling:
3 eggs	2 cups whipping cream
4–6 T hot water	1/4 cup sugar
2/3 cup sugar	1 tsp vanilla extract
1 tsp vanilla extract	approx. 1 1/4 cups raspberries
1/2 cup flour	2–3 T almond slivers
1/4 cup cornstarch	
1/2 tsp baking powder	

- Preheat oven to 400°–450° F.

- Make basic spongecake batter (see p. 74) from the ingredients given. Distribute batter evenly on a lined baking sheet. Place baking sheet in oven and bake approx. 17-23 minutes.

- Invert spongecake onto a kitchen towel dusted with sugar. Wet the baking paper lining and gently remove. Using the towel, roll spongecake jelly-roll fashion to cool.

- For the filling, whip cream with sugar until stiff. Rinse raspberries, mash approx. 3/4 cup with a fork and fold into whipped cream. Fill approx. 1 1/2 cups of the mixture in a pastry bag.

- Unroll cake and spread with fruit cream. Roll jelly-roll fashion and place on serving plate.

- Dot cake with cream and remaining fruit to garnish.

Caramel-Cream Sauce / Karamelcremesosse (Salzburg)

- 1 1/2 T sugar
- 4 T water, 1 cup milk
- 1 tsp cornstarch
- 1 egg yolk

● Caramelize sugar until light brown and reduce with water. Add all milk except for 2 T; heat.

● Mix cornstarch with remaining milk and the egg yolk; stir into the caramel. Bring to a boil once.

Applesauce / Vorarlberger "Süesslaschnitz" (Vorarlberg)

- 6–7 medium baking apples
- 1/2 cup water
- 1/2 cup dry white wine
- 1/2 tsp ground cinnamon
- 1/4 cup sugar
- 2–3 T butter
- juice of 1/2 lemon

● Peel, quarter and core apples; slice thinly. Boil with water, wine, cinnamon, sugar and lemon juice until soft.

● Let cool slightly. Put through a food mill and save the cooking liquid.

● While stirring constantly, add butter and some of the liquid; heat, but do not boil.

Sacher Glaze / Sacherguss

- 1 cup sugar
- 1/2 cup water
- 2/3 cup dark bitter chocolate

● Boil sugar and water approx. 5 minutes; let cool slightly. Melt chocolate in a double-boiler; let cool. Stir into sugar solution until creamy.

ear Compote / /orarlberger "Birestock" (Vorarlberg)

1/2 lb fresh, ripe pears	1/4 cup sugar
cup water	2–3 T butter
'2 cup dry white wine	1–2 T sugar
ice of 1 lemon	2 T bread crumbs
nch of ground cinnamon	

Peel, halve and core ears.

Boil water, wine and ugar. Add lemon juice, nnamon and pears. team; fruit should still be m.

● Brown butter and sugar; add bread crumbs and cook mixture.

● Add pears with juice and cook until thick, stirring constantly.

'lum Jam / Powidl

.ower Austria)

oprox. 6 lb fresh, ripe rune-plums

Rinse, halve and emove pits from 6 lbs ripe ums. Place in a large pot nsed with cold water; do ot add sugar.

Bring to a boil, stirring ell. Reduce heat and simmer approx. 4–6 hours, stirring occasionally, until thick and dark.

● While hot, pour into jars, cool slightly and seal.

Our Tip:
If adding sugar to the plums, add approx. 1/3 cup per lb plums.

About the Recipes:
All recipes serve four persons. Some desserts serve more, as they are also popular entrées. The oven temperatures given are for ovens with top and bottom heat. For convection ovens, set approx. 50° F lower; baking times remain the same.

Abbreviations:
Following are some frequently used abbreviations:

lb	pound(s)
oz	ounce(s)
qt	quart(s)
T	tablespoon(s)
tsp	teaspoon(s)

Photo Credits:
Upper Austrian Power Plant AG Photo Archives, Linz: pages 21, 30; Fotostudio Teubner, Füssen: pages 5, 15, 19, 22, 24, 35, 59; Fotostudio Sattelberger, Füssen: page 25 Gusto, Vienna: pages 28, 31, 33; Sigloch Edition, Künzelsau: pages 39, 41, 44; Komplettbüro, Munich: pages 36, 42, 55, 62, 64, 69, 73, 83; Österreich Werbung, Vienna: page 47; Vitri-Corning GmbH, Mühltal: page 51; Dr. Oetker, Bielefeld: page 79; Knorr, Maizena, Heilbronn pages 87, 88; Tübke & Partner, Munich: page 13 Langnese Iglo, Hamburg: page 93; Siemens Elektrogeräte GmbH, Munich: page 57; Unilever, Hamburg: pages 11, 58, 80

The author and publishing company would like to express their thanks to the above organizations for providing an excellent assortment of photographic material.

Design & Production: Verlagsbüro Fritz Petermüller, Siegsdorf
Editorial Office: U. Calis, Munich
English translation: Mary Heaney MARGREITER
Typesetting: Agentur für Sat & Typographie, Grassau
Lithography: ColorLine, Verona
Printed by: New Print, Trent

Publishing Number: 1717
ISBN 3-85491-810-0

Fax 0043 (0)512/265561-8
e-mail: kompass@kompass.a
http://www.kompass.at
4th Edition 2003